A PRIVATE'S WAR

The recollections of Private Frank James, who served with the 1st Northamptonshire Regiment in France and Flanders during The Great War of 1914 to 1918.

Compiled and edited by his nephew Ron James.

Published by his great-niece Elizabeth Ingham.

Ron James

Other books by the same author:
Avenging in the Shadows, No 214 Squadron Royal Air Force (1989)
I was one of the Brylcreem Boys (2013)
Mercy Mission to Java (2013)
Winged Words, An Airman's Miscellany (2013)

First published 2013 by E Ingham

Copyright © The Estate of the late Ron James 2013.
All rights reserved. No part of this work may be reproduced or utilised in any form or by any means, electronic or mechanical, including photocopying, recording or by any information storage and retrieval system, without prior written permission of the publisher.

Photographs by Ron James and courtesy of the Imperial War Museum and Northamptonshire Regimental Museum.

ISBN-13: 978-1482090956
ISBN-10: 1482090953

ABOUT THE AUTHOR

Ronald A James 1923-1995

Ron James was born and raised in Northampton, England. During the Second World War he joined the Royal Air Force as a mid-upper gunner, where he completed two tours of operations. His first tour was with No 90 Squadron on Stirling bombers and his second tour was with No 214 Squadron, where he took part in 100 Group special countermeasures operations, flying on B-17 Fortresses.

After the war he served two years in South East Asia as Movements Control Officer, helping to release the prisoners of war and civilians still held in Indonesian prison camps.

Ron later worked in the commercial side of the engineering industry and owned a transport motel and a bookshop in Northampton. He was a keen amateur historian, publishing a history of 214 Squadron 'Avenging in the Shadows' in 1989.

His retirement was spent travelling, writing, gardening, playing golf and spending time with his wife Win, daughter Liz, son Steve and grandchildren Katie and Kieran. This book was completed a couple of years before his death and published posthumously by his daughter Elizabeth.

Ron James

ACKNOWLEDGEMENTS

With grateful thanks to Colonel Wetherall and Peter Wilson of the Northamptonshire Regimental Museum, Abington Park, Northampton, for their assistance in allowing me access to the books and records of the Regiment and helping in every way during my research.

Ron James

CONTENTS

	About the Author	iii
	Acknowledgements	iv
	Prologue	7
1	Early Days	9
2	Into Battle	22
3	Trench Life	41
4	On The Somme	59
5	The Final Years	86
	Epilogue	108
	Poems	110
	Appendix	112
	Index	114

Ron James

PROLOGUE

When I was young, about eight or nine years old, I used to listen to my uncles talking about their experiences in The Great War. To me they were very old men and the war that they talked about was in the distant past. Little did I realise then that their war was only as yesterday, a mere thirteen years or so back. Now, forty-five years after my own war finished, I understand why the terrible events that these uncles were part of remained so fresh in their memories.

Frank James was just one of the many thousands of young men who flocked to the colours on the outbreak of war, to share in a moment of glory, worrying that the war would finish before they had had the opportunity to participate. The disillusionment came later!

In the few months preceding his death, I decided to make a note of Frank's wartime adventures and I had barely got started in writing them up before he died in 1987. However, with written reports of conversations I had with him and with the help of a tape recorder, I covered most of his experiences between 1914 to 1918.

Although Frank had an excellent recall of events that had taken place, they did not follow in chronological order and it was necessary to research the regimental history to put them in their proper perspective. Some of the incidents mentioned in this narrative I was unable to authenticate and I only have Frank's word for it, but in all other respects these notes follow on closely to those recorded in the official records.

The reason for writing this book was for my own satisfaction, as a student of military history and to pass on a copy to my children and grandchildren. It is not my intention to glorify war, in fact quite the reverse; to show the futility of it all and to show how a handful of people holding the reins of power can start off a chain of events that can bring death and destruction to millions of others.

Ron James
Northampton, 1990

A photograph of the James family taken at Hunsbury Hill cottages in 1898.
Back row: eldest son Will.
Second row: father George, mother Mary, Lil.
Front row: Fred, Frank, baby Arthur, Alice, Elsie.

1. EARLY DAYS

I was born in a small cottage in Kislingbury, Northamptonshire, in the year 1895. I doubt very much that there was any great celebration on my arrival, for although my mother and father were poor in a monetary sense, one thing that they did not lack was children. My father, George, at that time was working as a labourer in the sand pits at Milton and earning a very small wage. In fact, throughout his working life he earned very little money but I cannot at any time remember him getting into debt, which was something of a feat considering the large family he had to provide for.

Dad's father, Job, and the rest of his family had emigrated to the United States of America in the 1860s and like many other emigrants, had improved their standard of living and wanted the rest of their kin to share their good fortune. Money was sent over for dad's passage, but he decided against going even though a house and job were promised. I think probably the reason for dad turning the offer down was that he was married at the time and mother had strong family ties and persuaded him against making a move. Mother's twin sister lived in the next village and they were inseparable.

In those days large families were the norm. Both my parents had many brothers and sisters and if you went into a neighbouring village you could be sure of meeting up with some aunt, uncle or cousin.

Mary, my mother, never seemed to be out of childbirth when I was young. If she had heard of birth control she certainly never practiced it, as children arrived with monotonous regularity! In the end we finished up with four boys and five girls, not counting those who died in infancy.

One good thing that can be said of those childhood days was that although we were very poor and the younger children wore the hand-me-down clothes of their older brothers and sisters, we never went hungry as our parents always gave priority to our inner needs. I really think that because I had a good diet in my formative years I was able to survive the hardships that came later when I was serving in the trenches.

My two earliest childhood memories were of dad riding off on his penny-farthing bike and of my mother's visit to her parents who lived in Stowe Nine Churches, some miles from our cottage in Kislingbury. She pushed my brother Arthur in the pram and I walked along beside her. Even to this day I remember dragging myself along, hardly able to put one step in front of the other, and mother encouraging me with: "It's only a short way now Frank, we'll soon be there." A great walker was mother, even in late middle age she would think nothing of a ten mile hike!

Some time later we moved away from Kislingbury to Hunsbury Hill as dad managed to get a job as a furnace man at the ironworks there. The furnaces were owned by Pickering Phipps, a member of the well known local brewing family. A house went with the job so we moved into one of the six terraced cottages which stood just outside of the furnaces. *(After the second world war Blackwood Hodge & Company bought the site and these cottages, which stood in front of the main gate, were demolished.)*

We enjoyed the time we spent at Hunsbury Hill and after a while got friendly with the local landowners and farmers, who occasionally gave us the odd job to do, for which we were sometimes rewarded. One of my brothers, Fred, was really taken by the farming life; he was virtually adopted by one farmer and it was not long before he moved away from home and went to live in the farmhouse with the farmer and his family.

As I mentioned earlier, dad always made sure that we were well fed and he kept two allotments, one at Danes Camp and the other off the Towcester Road. Apart from vegetables, he also kept a pig and a few chickens and if you had visited our cottage you would have seen an amazing sight - instead of pictures on the wall, flitches of bacon would be seen wrapped in brown paper, whilst hams in pillowcases would be suspended from the ceiling!

Some years later we moved from Hunsbury Hill and went to live in Oxford Street, Far Cotton, by which time I had left school. At the age of thirteen I went to work for a jobbing builder who had his premises at the bottom of Bridge Street.

In those pre-war days life was much more leisurely. We worked hard and you could say that we were poorly paid, but I am sure we got more out of life than youngsters do these days. With no radio or TV we made our own amusements with the emphasis mainly on sport. People had more time for you too, always passing the time of day or stopping for a friendly chat - not that everything in the garden was rosy, for the divisions within society were much greater. On the one side would be the rich and professional classes (which included the clergy, doctors and landowners, etc.) and on the other would be the working classes. This all changed of course after 1918. Due to the losses incurred during the war and with the privations suffered by both officers and men, attitudes changed and outlooks altered so that things were never the same again.

The Great War, which started in August 1914, took this country by surprise, unlike the 1939 - 1945 war when most people were aware a year or two beforehand that conflict with Hitler's Germany was inevitable. Even when the other great powers were mobilising their armies, we had no idea that we would be drawn into war. Britain was totally unprepared, being both short of trained soldiers and munitions. But they were not short of volunteers! Men reported to the recruiting offices in their thousands within a few days of war being declared. I remember that my mates and I could hardly get to the barracks quick enough to enlist, for we wanted our share of the glory and were concerned that it might all be over before we could take part.

In the event the war continued for four years or more and those of us who survived came to regret that first flush of patriotic fervour which condemned us to the living hell of the trenches.

It was on 7th August that I enlisted, three days after war

was declared and I joined the 1st Battalion of the Northamptonshire Regiment. Unfortunately my two mates had joined up the previous day so we did not end up in the same company.

Both my friends were Far Cotton lads: 'Noggy' Bray, who lived in Thirlstane Road, and Arthur Worley who lived in Abbey Street. One other pal, Frank Roberts of Oxford Street, also joined a little later but sadly he lost his life early on in the war, at Neuve Chapelle in March 1915.

One of my brothers, Will, was already serving in the Forces, having joined at an early age. He was much older than the rest of us and had already seen service in South Africa. When the war started he was on holiday in Blackpool, having just received leave from his regiment, the King's Dragoon Guards (at that time based in Scotland). I never expected that I would see him for some considerable time but I happened to be at Northampton Castle Station when a train pulled in and he was on it! It appeared that he was joining a new regiment in London - the Life Guards. We were not destined to meet again until after the war, although on one occasion on the Western Front I had news of him at a camp near to where I was staying and I only missed him by a matter of minutes.

Dad soon followed Will into active service due to the fact he was a member of St John Ambulance and a reservist, so he left home almost immediately and I did not see him again until I returned in 1919.

As for my other two brothers, Arthur and Fred, Arthur followed me a few weeks later when he joined the Northamptonshire Yeomanry at the age of sixteen but luckily was never posted overseas. (It is my belief that his commanding officer was aware of his true age and kept him off the drafts.) Fred enlisted later and went into the Grenadier Guards.

At the end of August I left Northampton by train, along with many other keen recruits, to our first camp a short distance from Weymouth. We were under canvas in a field and as the weather was fine and warm we found it no hardship - more like being in the Boy Scouts! Although we were now in the Army, our equipment was practically nil. We paraded and marched in our civilian clothes and the only rifles we saw were in the hands of the instructors. (These were used for demonstration purposes only.) It was drill, route march and more drill most of the time. One of our favourite spots was the range at Wool, some eight miles away, but suffice to say we never had the opportunity to try out our skills with a rifle on the range itself.

Eventually we were issued with a uniform, which was a nice navy blue colour. When in November khaki became available, we thought how drab it seemed and were sorry to lose our original issue.

It was in November that a consignment of rifles arrived and it was decided that we would have a practice on the sea front at Weymouth. Cardboard cut-outs were made and these were placed on the sea shore so that all firing would be out to sea and not endanger anyone. Little did I realise that the fifteen rounds I fired then would be the only ones I would use before facing the enemy in battle!

At the end of the month our superiors decided we were now fit and able to take on the enemy, so we were granted seven days embarkation leave. Those seven days passed only too quickly and in a short time our intrepid band of volunteers were assembling for embarkation at Southampton. That winter day was very cold and I remember having to wait around a long time before going aboard. The ship was packed with troops and our contingent finished up in a very exposed position on the top deck. The ship was accompanied by two destroyers to protect us from any lurking U-Boat that might be around. Indeed, we did have one such alarm and stopped in mid channel with all the lights out. However, no attack was made on us and we sailed on to Le Havre without further incident.

The ironworks where my father worked, owned by Pickering Phipps.

Hunsbury Hill cottages where I lived as a child in 1898. These have now been demolished. The families who lived there were from left to right: Warwick, James, Johnson, Deacon, Furniss, Birch.

Me, Frank James, Northamptonshire Regiment 1914.

My father, George James, a reservist in St John Ambulance.

My brother Fred James, Grenadier Guard.

My eldest brother, Will James, of the Life Guards.

My friend Alf Matthews, myself and younger brother Arthur James (Northamptonshire Yeomanry).

A recruiting poster of 1915, typical of those that were published during the Great War.

Off to Bridge Street Station, a familiar scene in Northampton during the war.

2. INTO BATTLE

After a freezing and seasick passage we arrived at our destination in the cold dawn of a December morning, tired and in need of a nice warm bed. But no such luck! Like many soldiers before and since, we had to stand in line waiting for further orders to despatch us to some unknown distant place in a foreign land.

Eventually our transport arrived by courtesy of the French Railways. We had been allocated cattle trucks! These wooden-sided waggons had one large sliding door in the centre and were used for general freight and, as we discovered, troops too. (I travelled several times later on the French Railways and only once do I remember being on a passenger train, and that was when I was wounded and on my way to a military hospital.) On this particular journey forty-four men with all their equipment were allocated to each waggon and it took hours to reach our destination due to the train stopping and starting. At times we often got off to stretch our legs.

The camp we arrived at was Etaples, commonly known as 'Etaps'. It was a large bivouacked area near the sea and covered several acres. Its purpose was to hold and give further training to troops fresh out from England then send them off to join their various units in the battle zone. Our stay here was quite short. We did no training but were issued with extra equipment, one item being a goatskin jacket with all the hair still on it. We certainly looked a motley bunch with our coats of different colours! Later we found that with all the mud around it was better to wear these with the hair on the inside.

A few days later we continued on our rail journey, first to Arras and from there to a forward area near Givenchy where the 1st Northants were holding part of the line. We found that the battalion was somewhat depleted, for it had suffered many casualties a few days earlier whilst trying to recapture positions lost by neighbouring Indian troops. The weather too had played its part, being particularly severe with rain and snow nearly all the time. Under these conditions men were being invalided out with 'trench foot' and other ailments, so our draft was welcomed with open arms.

When we arrived in the trenches the war on the Western Front had reached a stalemate, for at the end of 1914 the German offensive had run its course due to the determined resistance of the British and French Armies. A continuous barrier was constructed which ran from the North Sea to the Swiss border and this altered the mobile character of the war.

Thus began the long, hard slogging match of trench warfare — the so called 'War of Attrition', which would claim the lives of millions of young men in the months and years that followed.

Even though the Germans were unable to make further headway, they ensured that their new positions would be superior to those of their enemies. By giving ground in some sectors and taking it in others, by throwing in relentless attacks, they established much better positions on the higher, drier ground of Flanders. These early operations gave our enemies a definite advantage over us and proved costly to the Allies in the battles still to come.

Our first experience of the Front Line was shattering. We expected that there would be some sort of order and organisation but instead we found no trenches, only a collection of shell-holes which were mostly filled with water. The mud and the rain dampened our spirits and we wondered what we had let ourselves in for.

In view of the low ground that we were occupying, it was impossible to dig trenches as you struck water about four inches down, so we had to go out at night with sandbags filled with earth and try and build parapets on top of the shell-holes. This measure did offer some protection against enemy fire.

The German positions were quite some distance from our own and I should imagine that they had the same sort of difficulties as we did. One thing was certain, both sets of defences were lightly held so things were generally quiet.

At night we sent out patrols to contact our neighbours in the line, an undertaking which usually took some fifteen to twenty minutes. (I believe the company we used to meet up with was the West Kents.)

After only a short spell at Givenchy we were taken out of the line and sent to Bethune on rest. Bethune was a small town not far behind the front and it still had its civilian population, so we did manage to relax and get drink and better things to eat at the local estaminets. I think it true to say that most of the money I spent in France was on food. The rations we were supplied with in the trenches were very poor and usually cold, so I made up for it when I was back in the rest areas. As for drinks, I was never interested in wine or spirits as these never appealed to me.

Our next move was not back to our last sector but to a place called Guinchy, only a short distance from Bethune. It was known as 'The Railway Triangle', for here was the junction of the main railway line between Lille - La Bassée - Bethune.

Before we had hardly settled into our new positions, I became a casualty of war! A piece of shrapnel from a German shell went into my boot. Fortunately for me this flying missile was at the end of its journey so it did no great damage. However, when I came to inspect my foot, it had swelled up like a balloon and I was unable to put my boot back on again. I reported to the Medical Officer and he sent me out of the line to a forward hospital not too far back, just behind our reserve trenches.

The 'hospital' consisted of a few tents in a field. Strangely enough, most of the patients at the hospital seemed to be unwounded and when I enquired I was told that they were suffering from trench foot, pneumonia, heart trouble, etc. The fellow in the next bed to me said that he had palpitations of the heart. It was not until later that I found that this condition could be self-induced. I often wondered whether this particular soldier was 'swinging the lead'. As far as I was concerned, I thought my minor wound well worth a spell in hospital with nice dry surroundings and decent food.

It was towards the end of January that I reported back for duty, just in time to come under mortar fire from 'Jerry' as he prepared for an assault on our lines. As it turned out, the attack was not carried out with any strength and we had no trouble in beating it off, although we did lose some of the lads through the mortar bombardment. Later, during the night, our relief arrived and we marched back to Bethune for rest and further battle training. This training lasted throughout the month of February. We all guessed of course that this prolonged period of instruction was for some purpose and we soon found out what it was to be when we entered the line two miles south of Neuve Chapelle.

This was one of the few times that our generals got it right when launching an offensive. Guns, men and munitions had been secretly brought up at night and carefully concealed. We even sent out wiring parties into No Man's Land to give the appearance that we were building up our defences in case of an attack.

One night I was picked for a covering party with another chap named Greenwood who came from Wellingborough. It was our job to protect the rest of our platoon, who were putting up barbed wire. It was a frightening experience as we had to lie up close to the enemy front line and could hear the Germans talking, even smell the smoke from their cigars! The situation was in no way improved when the 'Very' lights went up and exposed every detail of the terrain. I have heard it said that if you stood motionless you would not be seen, but I don't think this was the case. My belief was that the Germans often had their own men out there as well and did not wish to start a fire-fight in case they got shelled by us. Perhaps most of all, when the lights went up, it took some time to adjust their eyes and bring their weapons to bear.

Early morning on 10th March German aircraft appeared out of the mist and strafed our trenches at low level so we guessed that we had been rumbled at last, but this was soon forgotten when the guns opened up. It was the first time I had seen an artillery barrage and it was tremendous! The guns were mainly French 75s and although it would be untrue to say that they stood wheel to wheel, they were very close together.

Looking over the top of the trench you could see the enemy's forward lines erupting in a seething mass of debris, smoke and clods of earth. The noise was ear-shattering. When we climbed up over the parapet and into No Man's Land it was hard to imagine how anyone could have survived the scene of devastation that was in front of us. All too soon did we discover that our optimism was ill-founded as Jerry's artillery started to range in on us and, almost unbelievably, rifle fire started up from the front line trenches!

My participation in this action soon ended when I felt a heavy blow to my arm and I realised that I had been wounded. Dropping to the ground, I checked to see what damage had been done. I found that I had stopped another piece of shrapnel, so I decided that it would be best to return to our own lines. Crouching and crawling, I managed to make my way back to our own lines, then a long walk ensued in search of a medic. I probably travelled three or four miles before coming across a medical officer who was installed in a dugout. He treated my arm with iodine, put on some lint and a bandage, then sent me back up the line.

The battle continued for another two days. Although we took some of our objectives and captured many prisoners, our own losses were great with 12,000 casualties. The 'Steelbacks', the Northants 2nd Battalion, were decimated, losing 431 officers and men, with only 4 officers and 180 men surviving the action.

After the war had finished and the various battles were analysed, it was found that we should have beaten the Germans but faulty staff work and failure to bring up reserves at the right time gave the Germans the opportunity to bring up reinforcements and stop any further advance. Sad to say, mistakes of this kind continued as the war progressed and we seemed to learn little from our experiences!

By the third day my arm had swollen out of all proportions. My fingers were like sausages and the flesh around my wrist was cutting into my tunic. The Medical Officer took one look at it and sent me off to hospital. This was easier said than done, for it was quite a walk back to railhead where I was to meet the hospital train and I was in some agony! I don't know how I made that journey I was so light-headed, but at least when I did arrive the train that was in operation was a normal passenger one and I had a seat to sit in. On this train was a full contingent of medical staff, which included British nurses.

One of the nurses noticed my distress and asked, "Are you in pain?"

I replied, "I think I am going to die." With that she went off and later returned with a doctor.

The doctor took a look at my arm then told the nurse to find a chair, which she did. I was then seated on this chair and the nurse held my head back; the doctor meanwhile sat on my lap. Next he put my arm between his arm and body and with a knife cut into my arm to release the pressure that had built up and also to get rid of some of the poison. All this happened of course without the aid of anaesthetic, but the shape I was in it hardly mattered. Afterwards I remembered very little and it is possible that I had been given a shot of morphia.

When I eventually regained my senses I found myself looking out of a second floor window of a hospital in Rouen, gazing on a statue of Joan of Arc.

Three weeks passed before I was fit enough to join the battalion again. They were now holding part of the line near Festubert. In this sector there were no trenches as such, rather a collection of sandbag barricades as the ground was waterlogged and resembled a swamp! No work could be done during daylight but at night working parties went out with sandbags filled with dirt to add a bit more protection. Fortunately for us this was a quiet sector and our nightly excursions raised no reaction from Jerry.

At the beginning of May the battalion came out on rest and to begin special training. The area we now occupied was much like a battleground, which of course was the object of the exercise as it was meant to be as realistic as possible. For many hours every day we practised bayonet drill, bomb throwing and attacking or defending certain parts of the terrain. It seemed something of a relief after our spell in the trenches and I don't suppose many of us took it too seriously.

One incident I remember well was during bayonet drill. Our instructor was Sergeant Short who lived in Cambridge

Street. (*Years later he became a physical training instructor with the local police.*) He must have seen a grin on my face, for he called me out and said, "When I say point, you point, and when I say parry, you parry!"

He had hardly got the words out of his mouth before he caught me with the butt of his rifle in the chest and put me flat on my back. It certainly hurt! Being quick tempered, I swore at him. This did not go down well in front of the men and I knew by the look on his face that in the future I had better watch out.

His revenge was not long in coming, for on the following morning, whilst on parade during inspection, he said, "James, you are unshaven and I am putting you on report."

Later in the morning I was marched up in front of the CO, Captain Dickson, who asked me, "What excuse have you for not shaving?"

I replied, "I've never used a razor in my life."

He came over to me and felt my chin and said, "You should be home with mother."

To this I replied, "If it can be arranged Sir".

He gave a wry smile and dismissed the charge - a fine man was Captain Dickson.

On May 5th we were on the march. Although the war may have been at a static stage, it seemed that we were continually on the move - in the line, in support, in reserve or out on rest, so that for half of the time we did not know where we were. However, on this occasion we found ourselves in familiar surroundings – in the trenches before Aubers Ridge, less than two miles from where we had fought our last battle at Neuve Chapelle.

The lessons that had been learnt from the attack on Neuve Chapelle were put to good use by the Germans. They realised that a breakthrough here would put their bases at Lille and La Bassée in jeopardy and threaten their lines of communication to the coast, so defences on the ridge were strengthened. Concrete was used extensively in the forward positions and the parapets were able to withstand fire from our twelve pounder guns. Also, loopholes were made in these parapets at ground level for the use of machine-guns, which had already been carefully sited to sweep our front line. Another innovation was that machine-gun pits were dug in No Man's Land so that firing would be at ground level, with fields of fire that would enfilade any attacking force trying to cross the 300 yards which separated the two lines of trenches.

On the British side, the High Command made a terrible mistake in not giving the infantry adequate artillery support. At Neuve Chapelle it had been used in strength and was successful, but at Aubers Ridge our guns in lesser numbers failed to make any impression on the enemy defences or neutralise the German heavy artillery batteries. Perhaps most importantly, in view of the short distance of ground to be covered, was the inability to break down the enemy wire.

The attack on the ridge was scheduled for the early hours of May 8th and B Company (to which I belonged), jointly with D Company, would lead the attack. For some reason or another it was postponed for twenty-four hours. It was rumoured that two men in khaki had been caught in No Man's Land, who turned out to be German spies. This I should say was a lot of bunk, for being overlooked from the higher ground, Jerry must have been aware of our intentions, what with all the activity that was taking place beyond our lines, and was well prepared to stave off an imminent attack.

In the front line trench we could hardly move with all the equipment gathered there: scaling ladders, bridging material, planks, wire cutters, etc. For myself, I was issued with a bomber's apron and a supply of Mills bombs. In a training session previously the instructor found that I had a good throwing arm, so to my dismay I had landed a most unsavoury job - one that meant I would be one of the first over the top in the morning.

Throughout the night the NCOs (Non Commissioned Officers) came round to us dishing out a rum ration, one tablespoonful per man, and I suppose during this wait we had five or six visits. Personally, I had tried rum once and it had nearly choked me, so I always refused after that. It is my belief that the rum ration cost many men their lives, for by going over the top 'half-cut' they made the wrong decisions. In this particular battle, men who were wounded tried to stagger to their feet only to be hit again, whereas if they had remained where they had fallen they would probably have survived.

The morning dawned bright and clear with the promise of being a nice day and a stillness prevailed along the line, shortly to be broken when the opening salvos from our guns started to fall on the enemy's back areas. After half an hour the bombardment switched to the German front and support trenches and this was the prelude for our entry into the fray.

Behind us we had a battery manned by the 23rd London Artillery Company, which I believe was a territorial unit. Their first shell fell behind our breastworks killing a lot of our own lads, the second was into No Man's Land and they finally found the target with the third.

It was now our turn to go into action so we clambered over the parapet and made our way at walking pace towards the Jerry trenches. The ground we initially had to cover was fairly flat, intersected by small streams and an occasional ditch, and close to the enemy wire there was a dyke approximately twelve feet wide. The noise of battle was deafening and as I went forward, encumbered with the extra weight of the bombs I was carrying, it occurred to me that with all the explosives around my body I was a walking time bomb, so I decided to ditch them in a shell-hole.

After only a few minutes our guns ceased firing. I suppose by that time we had progressed half way across No Man's Land and that was when the Germans opened up on us. It was hard to say what was happening behind me for I was up front and when you are in a situation like that you seem detached from your mates and very much on your own.

I was coming up to the big dyke and, looking past it, I saw that the wire was still intact and wondered how I was going to get through it. I need not have worried for this problem soon solved itself for me as I received a violent blow on the arm which spun me round and put me on the ground - I was wounded once more!

As I lay on the ground facing the German line, wondering what my next move would be, the rest of the lads (or what was left of them) were passing me by. Only a few got as far as the wire because the Maxims (German machine-guns) were taking their toll and men were going down in swathes. Someone fell almost on top of me. I was unable to tell if he was dead or badly wounded but I did notice that his body twitched several times and this may have been caused by further bullets hitting him.

Across the dyke and leaning over the rim, I saw my brother-in-law's brother, also wounded, and as he lay there I saw a bullet or piece of shrapnel take off one of his ears. I learned later that he had died.

Although I could feel blood running down my arm, I kept motionless for I knew it would be suicide to make a move. In all I spent fourteen and a half hours playing dead. My survival was probably due to the body which fell alongside me, screening me from the enemy's fire. All around I could hear moans and cries of the wounded, some calling for their mothers or wives whilst others cursed the Germans with their dying breath. It was a nightmare! No one could do anything about it. Everywhere there were piles of both dead and dying, looking from a distance like so many sheep huddled together in a field.

Our opening barrage had been a complete failure and left the Germans almost unscathed. The speed with which their Maxim machine-guns were put into action had resulted in the massacre of our troops. At no point did we manage to break into the enemy lines and after the early slaughter the Germans focussed their attention on those of us who were wounded and lying out on the battlefield. This was a new departure from the norm since there was a sort of tactical agreement that anyone 'hors de combat' would be spared further wounding. It sometimes happened that stretcher bearers would be allowed to pick up casualties out in No Man's Land without interference - but not on this day. To make matters worse the German guns started to put down a barrage on our front and support lines, so there was no alternative but to stay where we were and hope the firing would die down.

During the day other regiments tried to make a breakthrough but they suffered the same fate as ourselves. Only when darkness fell were we able to crawl our way back to our own lines. It had been a terrible ordeal. Most of us had spent fourteen hours or more in the open, exposed to enemy fire the whole time!

At roll call the next day it was found that of the 776 officers and men who took part in the action, only 64 returned, and amongst those who lost their lives was our CO, Captain Dickson.

It was another spell in hospital for me, but this time it was more acceptable because my arm was not too badly damaged. After it had healed and I had returned to the battalion, which was now at Bethune on rest and reorganisation, I was given 'Blighty' leave.

To return to Northampton after the trenches was like entering into a new world. Things had changed little since I had left and although it had only been a matter of a few months, to me it seemed like a lifetime. There was an air of optimism around and most people you spoke to expected that the war would be over by Christmas. In the shops there was no rationing and goods seemed plentiful; the only difference I found was that most of my friends were away, having joined the Services.

I did find it difficult to discuss the war with people at home, for they had read glowing reports in the newspapers of our successes in France (often written by people who called themselves observers and who had never left their seat in some London newspaper office). How could you tell people full of hope that we were not winning the struggle and, with the stalemate that then existed, that there was no end in sight? Even if I had mentioned the situation at the Front, I doubt that I would have been believed, for the propaganda given out by the press had done its work and no doubt I would have been labelled a defeatist. You have to remember that in those days practically all news was put out by the newspapers, as the wireless was in its infancy and not available to most people.

Paradoxically, as it may appear, my experiences in France created an invisible barrier between myself and the folk at home. I felt somewhat alienated and realised that the only people I could relate to were my mates back in the trenches. It would have been unfair to tell your parents of the hardships you were having to endure in the trenches, of the hundreds of dead and wounded in your battalion, of the vermin, the mud and of the cheapness of human life, so easily squandered by our generals in futile attacks that did nothing but take a few yards of ground. I kept silent and shunned any talk of war.

Although it was marvellous to be back home, I found it most difficult to relax and wind down. One day when I was feeling a bit bored, I went to visit my brother Arthur, who was with the Northants Yeomanry stationed at Towcester. I managed to see his commanding officer, who was a very decent chap, and he consented to give my brother the day off. Together we went to visit our other brother Fred, who was working for a farmer named Griffin on Hunsbury Hill.

Fred lent us his shotgun and we went round the fields to see if we could bag a few rabbits for the pot. I don't think we were lucky that day, but I remember being approached by a young man in civvies who said, "You are trespassing on Pickering Phipps land. Hand over that gun."

Whether we were on his land or not I don't know, but both Arthur and myself were in uniform and this chap of our age was ordering us to hand over the gun. My temper was already at simmering point and I said to him, "If you don't get out of the way, the only part of this gun you will be getting will be out of the barrel!"

If Arthur had not intervened I think that I would have attacked him, but he saw the mood I was in and beat a hasty retreat.

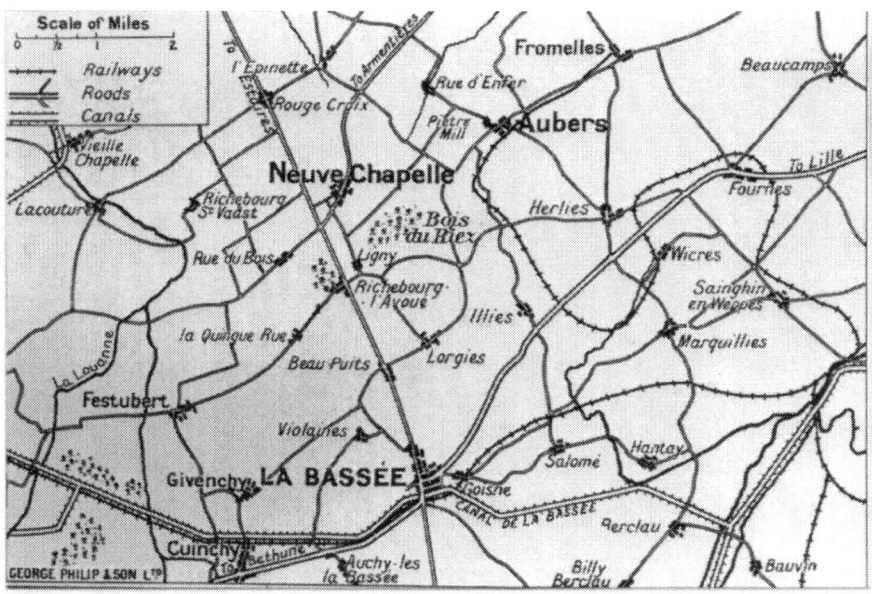

Map showing the close proximity of the two major battles of 1915 in which Frank took part - Neuve Chapelle and Aubers Ridge.

Afternoon tea – the engine-driver supplies the hot water. With the many stops on the French railways during the war it took the trains many hours to reach their destinations. Notice the goatskin jackets issued to the soldiers for winter warfare.

Into No Man's Land. The explosion was probably caused by a mine going up and the troops rush in to occupy the crater.

British artillery on the Western Front.

A forward hospital tending to the wounded. Notice the handcart for moving casualties.

How the barbed wire gets there. An officer leads a wiring party to the front line.

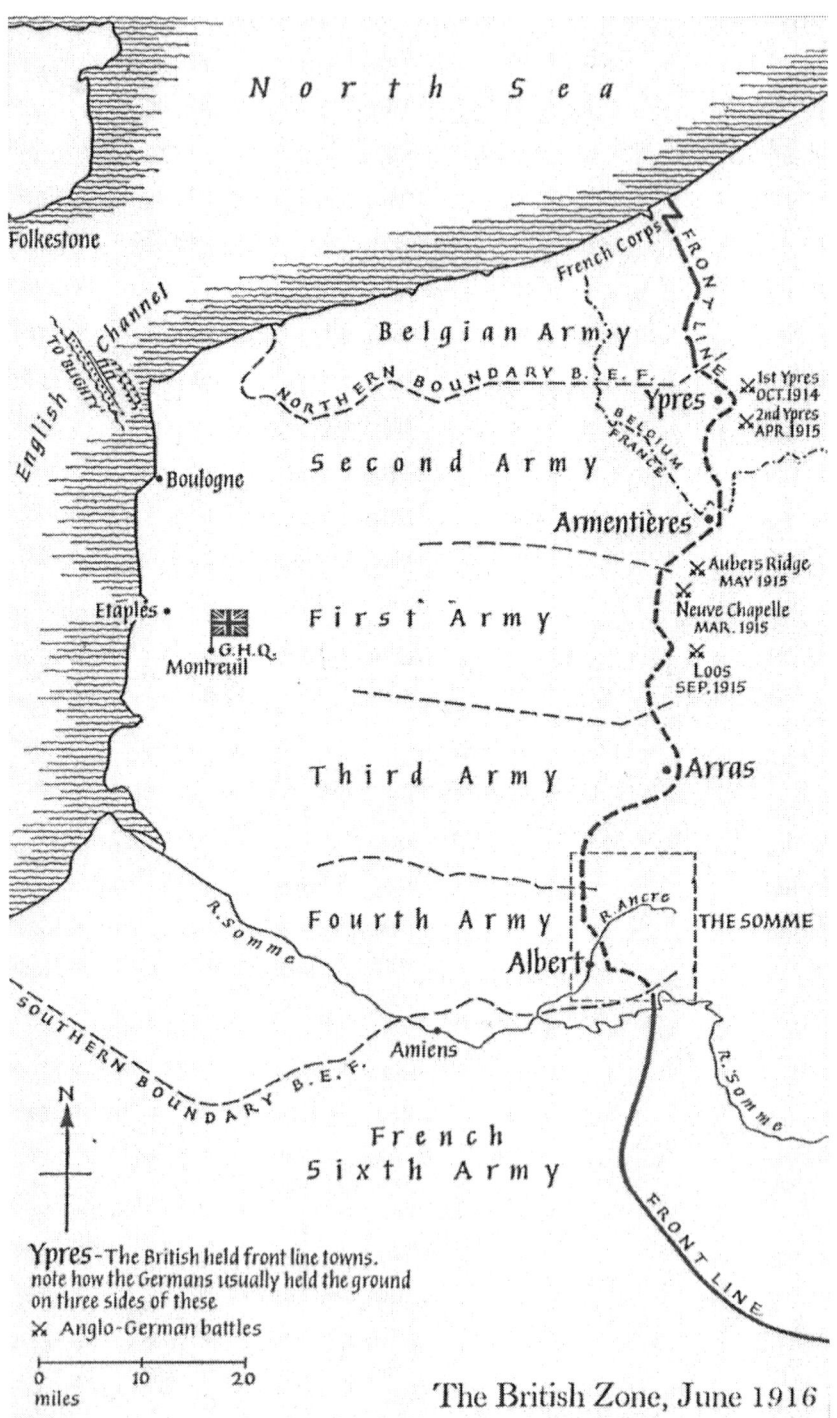

The British Zone, June 1916

3. TRENCH LIFE

In the previous chapter I made mention of the fighting in which the 1st Northants were involved, but it gave only scant details of the everyday life we spent in and out of the trenches. My likes and dislikes were probably shared by thousands of other soldiers, but no record of World War One would be complete without reference to the perils and hardships suffered by the men up front at the sharp end of war.

Trenches

The Western Front was a gigantic trench system which stretched from the North Sea in Belgium through France and up to the Swiss border, a distance of some 400 miles. At first, in the year 1914 and early 1915, the defences in some sectors consisted only of shell-holes and breastworks but later, through the efforts of millions of the protagonists working like ants night and day, networks were made which extended many miles in depth.

By the middle of 1916 these defences were formidable and instead of one, you would find three parallel trenches: the front line, the support trench and the reserve line, all of which were connected by communication trenches. Back in the rear would be the artillery and beyond them the rest areas where troops would be billeted when out of the line.

If the battlefield could be seen from the air, the trenches would have resembled the edge of a saw with its serrated teeth, and each tooth would have been a fire-bay which held six men. Outside the front trenches, barricades of barbed wire would have been placed to give added protection in case of an attack, whilst No Man's Land would have looked very much like the face of the moon with its cratered surface. One other feature would have been the debris of war which was scattered everywhere, amongst which would lie the unburied dead of both armies.

In winter No Man's Land was a terrible place to gaze on - a scene of desolation with spectral shell-shattered trees and quagmires awaiting to trap the unwary who ventured out into its terrain. Late spring and summer showed a different aspect entirely with wild flowers blooming, grass and even cultivated crops like wheat covering up the many scars of war. Sometimes even the shell-torn trees burst into life and leaves appeared upon their gaunt frames, whilst skylarks and other songbirds could be heard above the sound of the guns. It was at times like these that No Man's Land presented to the observer a paradox of both savagery and beauty.

Although battle with the enemy was not continuous, the battle to keep the trenches habitable certainly was. Most of our time was taken up with filling sandbags, improving parapets, putting duck-boards down and building sumps to run off the water underfoot. Shelling also added to our problems, as often whole sections of trench would be flattened and this meant we would have to work at night to repair it once again. This was a terrible job, working in darkness, not only digging up earth and mud but the dead bodies of your comrades as well! One added twist to this horrendous task was that the Germans, who had already ranged their machine-guns to sweep the top of our trenches with their fire, would open up without warning and claim further casualties.

In the German forward trenches there were usually deep dugouts, but this was not the case in our own; ours were further back in the support or reserve lines.

As previously mentioned, the men who manned the forward trench were placed in fire-bays, some twenty feet or so long and seven feet deep. Of the six men occupying the bay, two would be on sentry duty at any one time, which with rotation worked out two hours on and four off. Just before dawn everybody would 'stand-to' as this was the time that an attack usually took place. Once it was light we got the 'stand-down' and could relax once more. There was no shelter in the fire-bay but we did dig holes in the side to hold various articles. It always seemed cold and it was hard to keep warm and dry, especially with the mud and water which was always underfoot and many times over our feet as well.

Time spent in the trenches varied. If you were in a quiet sector it would perhaps be three days up front, three in support and six in reserve, but if there was a 'Push' on, you never knew when you would be pulled out. Once we spent twenty-eight days in the second line and our officer had a nervous breakdown, but normally you would be relieved after seven days or so.

Even when we were in the back areas it did not mean that we were excused duties and often these duties proved to be more perilous than sitting it out in the front line. It could entail a four mile march up to the front loaded down with supplies, or being sent out on a wiring party into No Man's Land. In fact, all working parties were dangerous as the enemy knew what we were up to at night and so shelled our back areas. Many of our men were lost on these nightly excursions.

Vermin

One of our off duty occupations was getting rid of lice. No one was exempt, we all had the same problem. It was impossible to keep yourself clean. We had lice in our hair, on our bodies, in our boots and even in our tin hats! If it was possible to light a candle we would run the flame up and down the seams of our clothes and there was hardly a spot free from lice or their eggs. As the flame reached the lice you would hear a 'pop, pop, pop' sound as the pests were destroyed. Of course, there was little we could do about our unwanted lodgers except keep their numbers down and after a time we got used to them, but if you happened to be in a dugout at night and got warm, they made life very unpleasant for you.

When we were out of the line we usually had access to a super-heated drying machine, which was very similar to a concrete mixer. We used to strip off, bundle up our clothes and put them in this machine and they came out nice and dry. I think it did the trick and killed off the lice, but it was only a matter of a few days before we were 'lousy as cuckoos' once more.

Rats were a different proposition entirely, some people like myself never worried about them, but I do admit that there was something obscene and repulsive when you saw these large, healthy-looking rodents running around and knowing what they had been feeding upon. At times the men did organise rat hunts to try and keep the infestation under some degree of control, but it was like spitting against the wind for all the good it did, for they were in too great a number for it to have any effect.

Cleanliness

You can well imagine that whilst in the line it was impossible to keep clean, as water was at a premium and had to be brought up from the back areas. This was for drinking only and was on ration. If any of us did shave, we used only rain water. All the time I spent in France, I only remember having two good baths and that was in a coal mine in the Bethune sector. The mine was derelict but fortunately we found the miners baths still in working order. At other times we did manage to get an occasional shower or a good wash down when out on rest.

Illness

Most people who served in the trenches suffered with sickness at some time or another. The two most common complaints were trench fever (caused by body lice) and trench foot (a type of frostbite brought on by having one's foot immersed in water over a long period). This latter complaint was frowned upon by the hierarchy, who considered it an offence and a sign of malingering. We used to have regular foot inspections and were issued with whale oil for protection, but even the most stringent of precautions failed to stop the condition. Wearing puttees (support bandages on the legs) did not help either, as standing in water made them shrink and cut off circulation to the feet. I think that wearing puttees then caused me to suffer badly with varicose veins in later life.

Self-inflicted Wounds

For some people life in the trenches was too much of a burden for them to bear and all types of subterfuge were practiced in order to get into hospital or go back home to 'Blighty'. Apart from the usual practice of shooting off a finger or toe, less drastic measures were employed. One such method was to hit the knee continually with a wet towel until it swelled up large, or to eat the cordite from a bullet, which was supposed to give palpitations of the heart. If these ploys proved successful they bought a little reprieve from the trenches - but only for a short time!

Deserters

Of course the most drastic step one could take was to desert. This brought with it the death penalty if caught - a sentence that was swiftly carried out after being found guilty by a Field Court Martial (see appendix).

One such incident that I can relate to happened in our battalion. The man in question, I believe, went absent before we went over the top at Aubers Ridge and was captured shortly afterwards. When he returned to us he was as black as soot. (He had either been working or living in a coal mine.) At the time of his capture we were living in pretty primitive conditions out on the line, with latrines out in a field covered round with hessian to give some sort of privacy. One night the prisoner asked his guard if he could visit the toilet, which was granted, so he went out to the latrine with his escort who kept watch outside the hessian screen. It is a mystery how the prisoner managed to keep a knife or blade upon his person, but by slitting down the sacking he made good his escape and disappeared under the cover of darkness. Nothing more was heard of the prisoner after he escaped, although it was rumoured that he had been recaptured and had managed to free himself for a second time.

The sequel to this saga happened back in Northampton in 1924. I was then working for the Gas Company and we were putting in a new main between Black Lion Hill and St. Andrews Road. At the time my mates and I were in conversation with two men working for the 'Borough'. Another man came up and joined them carrying two cups of tea - it was the same chap who had deserted in France! I took him aside and said, "How the bloody hell did you get out? I thought you were dead."

He laughed and replied, "Wouldn't you like to know. So would plenty of other people! And as for being dead, I very nearly was, several times." That was all I managed to get out of him.

During the years that followed, I saw him many times but never got into conversation except for passing the usual pleasantries that one would make on meeting an acquaintance in the street. When he died he was living in Gladstone Road on Spencer Estate, but I have never divulged his name to anyone as I thought it would be most unfair to members of his family who were still living.

Artillery

Our feelings towards gunners were mixed. We had very little time for the heavy artillery, who were well back from the front line, living in what we considered to be the 'lap of luxury' - good deep dugouts and better rations - and who sometime sent over 'short-falls' which killed our own men. The field artillery were liked a little better; they were placed just behind our lines and suffered casualties the same as we did when coming under fire from the enemy's guns. Then there were the artillery men who were in the line with us, manning the Stokes mortars; they shared the same dangers and hardships as ourselves and these men were accepted by us all.

Whatever the artillery did, they could never win as far as we were concerned. If they opened up on the enemy, we suffered from the counter-barrage and this initial shelling started off a chain of events that brought further losses to our ranks as the Germans retaliated and widened the conflict. We blamed them for many things: for not prolonging the shelling when we were called upon to make an attack; for the shells that dropped short and killed our own men; and for not destroying the enemy wire (which was probably our biggest moan of all). The accusations we made against our gunners were probably unfair though because, like the rest of us, they were only working to orders and were often short of ammunition and supplies.

Gas

My first experience of gas occurred during 1915. I remember that three of us were holding a derelict farm house when someone shouted "Gas!". We had been told that the best method to combat this was to urinate into a cloth and hold it to your nose. (Gas masks were only issued to us later in the war.) As I always carried a spare pair of socks with me, I used one of these as prescribed to ward off the gas and I will admit it worked alright for me.

The Germans used chlorine gas at first, which although nasty, was not as deadly as the phosgene and mustard which followed in the years to come. (*Brother Fred was blinded for three days when he came into contact with mustard gas.*)

British gas was used in conjunction with smoke and was more of a deterrent than a poison gas. It may not have been lethal but it could cause panic in the enemy's ranks when sent over prior to an attack being made.

One serious set-back in the use of gas as a weapon was that it could not be controlled and gave both friend and foe the same treatment if the wind veered. Mustard gas in its liquid form, lying out in No Man's Land amongst the craters and hollows, was no respecter of persons and blistered all and sundry. It also had the capacity to remain active over a long period of time.

Gas was a diabolical weapon. Not only did it kill and maim, but the thousands of men who had been exposed to it and had survived the war, suffered from its effects for the rest of their lives.

Rest and Recreation

When people think of the Great War they imagine that our soldiers spent ninety percent of their time in the trenches, but this was not the case. Short periods were spent in the front line but the rest of the time we were moved from place to place or were resting up in some back area. Sometimes after a battle in which we had lost a lot of men, the battalion would be sent back well out of the firing line to await fresh drafts sent over from England, to bring it up to strength once more. On the arrival of these reinforcements, a training programme would be started and it might be several weeks before we started on our stint of duty in the trenches again.

Once we were out on rest, various games were arranged for us - football, athletics and the like - between ourselves and other units. Talavera Day was always celebrated and we were often given days off to visit the estaminets in the nearby villages, where we could usually get a decent meal.

Rations

The food we had at the Front was pretty awful! It was usually stew brought up by horse cart and on the cart were four big 'dixies' which held about eight or nine gallons each. It was not often that the stew was hot and the meat was usually very fatty. If we were under fire, rations could only be brought up on the backs of men and were hours late.

Apart from hard boiled eggs, there was always soup and tea and we were never without our hard tack biscuits and plum jam. If it was possible, I used to boil up my biscuits and add the jam to make a sort of crumble. To eat the biscuits dry was an experience – they made your jaw ache and it was something of a feat to finish one off at one go.

Friend and Foe

The Germans: I never had any hate for the Germans. I believed that they were much like us; they had no say in the conduct of the war and were forced to obey orders. It is true that in some cases we disliked some regiments more than others. The Prussian Guard and Bavarians were the worst; they always seemed to be looking for trouble. When we were facing them in the line you could be sure of receiving plenty of rifle grenades and mortar fire.

The French: We had little contact with the French although we did feel that they were leaving the bulk of fighting to us at times. It was said that in the early years of the war they often left the trenches and went home for the weekend, but this was probably an exaggeration.

The Americans: Brash but likeable and good-natured. We never did consider them as good fighting men, but it did our morale no end of good when they appeared in strength towards the last stages of the war, bringing with them masses of supplies.

Thoughts at the time

We never got a clear picture of our situation and never knew whether we were winning or losing. Even the officers knew very little. We were shuffled about like chess men and had no idea where we were half the time. On the eve of an attack we might be told, "Just one big push lads and we will have Jerry on the run," but no mention was made of finishing the war. It is a wonder we kept as cheerful as we did. Of course we had our good and bad days but at no time did we envisage defeat. We knew that at some future date we would finish up on the winning side.

In 1918 the German soldiers were told that the Allies were on their knees and would soon seek submission, as the U-Boat campaign was bringing them down to starvation level and one final attack would end the struggle. Strange as it may seem, the very success of their Spring Offensive produced a reverse effect on their morale and this was probably an important factor in their final collapse.

The German population itself was in a poor way where food was concerned and their troops were on minimum rations. The speed of the German advance took the British completely by surprise and they had to abandon many of their warehouses and food dumps to the enemy. It is my belief that when the Germans saw the food and other supplies that were available to us they could not believe their eyes and, with the failure to defeat our army, they realised that they were a spent force and it would only be a matter of time before the growing strength of the Allies, now combined with the Americans, would bring about their demise.

A sentry on duty in the trenches. His periscope is camouflaged with sacking.

Dishing out the rations.

Well constructed officers quarters in Flanders, different from those of their counterparts in front line dugouts.

A German Officer's trench. In comparison with our troops the Germans lived almost in the lap of luxury. Some of their quarters were also fitted with electric light.

French soldiers showing the results of a rat hunt. The Poilu with his dog (below) had a field day.

A foot inspection by the Medical Officer.

Field Boot Repairers of 4th Northants Regiment.

The primitive gas masks used in 1915.

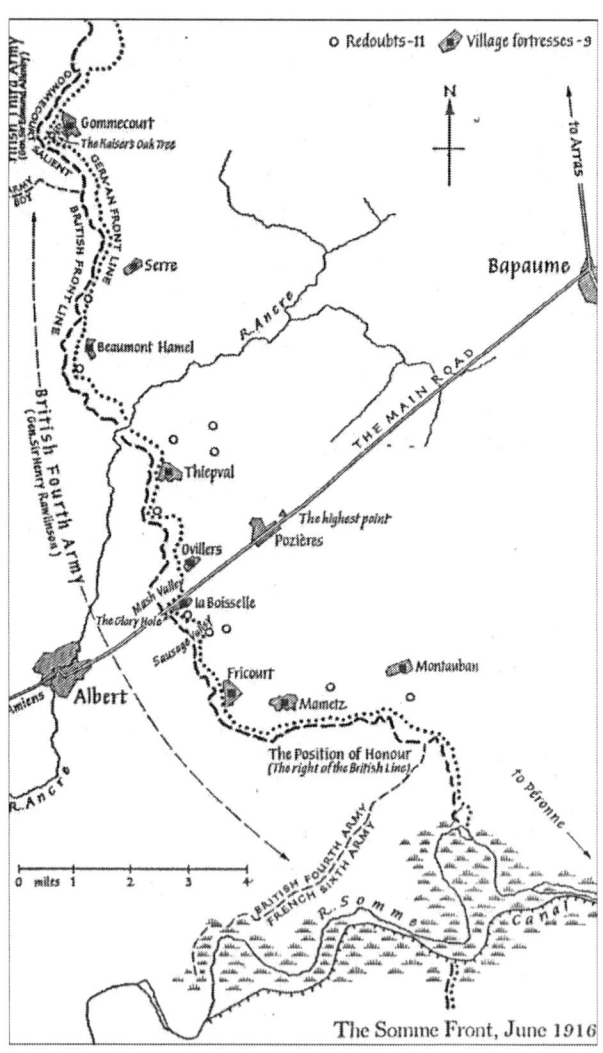

The Somme Front, June 1916

4. ON THE SOMME

When I returned from leave, I rejoined the battalion somewhere behind the lines near Loos and found them busily engaged in the construction of new support trenches. It was reported that a German attack was in the offing and we were strengthening our defences to meet it. Within days the plans were altered and in a flurry of activity saps were being pushed forward from the front line so that an advanced trench could be built. This of course could only mean one thing - we were going over to the offensive again!

It must have been apparent to the Germans that an attack of some sort would soon begin because our patrol activity increased, supplies and men came up from the rear and working parties were out at night. They soon retaliated against our men out on night work and their snipers and mortar fire claimed early victims.

To describe the countryside around Loos would be to liken it to some of the coal mining areas in South Wales, only more industrialised. Wherever one looked there were chimney stacks, mine machinery and large dumps. These dumps had changed the face of the landscape. Before mining had begun it would have been fairly flat, but throughout the years these gigantic slag heaps had arisen and made it into an undulating countryside.

In 1915 the miners and their families had left their homes to seek safer surroundings, leaving the fields fallow and the mines unoccupied. Apart from the network of trenches on the western side of the valley towards Loos (which was behind the German lines), there was little sign of a battle area - more of dereliction and decay.

One very unusual feature at Loos was the opposing front lines. Whereas the German positions were located amongst the slag heaps and showed up black; we were in a lower and less disturbed area, so when we excavated our trenches the soil was mainly chalk and it showed up white.

The so called 'Battle of Loos' opened on 21st September with an artillery barrage that lasted four days, both day and night. Even though Jerry was protected to some degree by his deep dugouts, it must have been a terrifying experience. Having been subjected to similar treatment, I know only too well the feeling of dread at the sound of each explosion.

Many of the men I served with proved their bravery time and time again in going over the top, but sustained bombardment of this sort turned them into shivering wrecks and broke their morale completely.

The early morning of the 25th was misty and dull and from our front trench arose a cloud of smoke and gas which drifted in a slight wind towards the enemy. Men in the first wave of the attack followed up shortly after and we could see them clambering over the parapet and disappearing into the mist. As we were in support that day, it was not until nearly two hours later that we were called upon to enter the fray. Meantime, the wind had changed slightly and we were getting a dose of our own gas.

The two battalions which had gone forward to lead the assault had made little headway due to the gas and heavy machine-gun fire and were bogged down in No Man's Land, so it was decided that the Royal Sussex and ourselves should make another attempt.

Our attack had all the makings of another Aubers Ridge disaster, the only difference this time being the gas. It is possible that we would have succeeded if the German wire had been broken, but we found it untouched so once again we had to seek shelter in the contours of the ground to avoid the intense rifle and machine-gun fire. Men of different regiments were all mixed together and it became a real shambles! The gas was lying in the shell-holes in the lower ground and choking the men who were looking for cover. Many panicked and cut and ran back towards their own lines, whilst the rest of us coughed and prayed that someone would find a way to rescue us from this predicament. The Germans were making hay of this situation and methodically concentrating their fire on the men in front of the wire. It was only a stroke of luck that saved us from being massacred.

Whilst our own private war had been taking place, other units of the 1st Division had made a successful breakthrough on our flank, thus getting round behind the Germans who were facing us, forcing them to retreat or surrender. If this had not happened few of us would have survived.

One of our officers in this action was awarded the Victoria Cross for his part in rallying the men in retreat and urging them forward again into the attack, but he lost his life when struck down by a sniper's bullet.

Loos was where the British Army used gas for the first time, not the noxious type favoured by the Germans but nasty all the same as it could incapacitate you for quite a considerable time. I will always remember that day, for we had to take as our objective a place called Lone Tree Farm - a small shattered tree standing by a rickety gate post.

After the fighting had died down in our sector, shortly after our rescue, several of the lads and I were detailed for a burial party. We found a very large shell-hole and put in the corpses after taking off their identity tags and any other personal items that they had on them. These we placed in the small haversacks we carried with us. After marking the grave we moved off to rejoin the rest of the battalion, which had continued to advance, and met up with them shortly before nightfall.

When they got through the enemy lines, the battalion had found the going much easier and advanced over one mile past their original objective, losing touch with other units. It was decided that we would wait until daybreak before making our next move, so we settled down on the ground trying to get some rest. We all spent a miserable night for the rain poured down in torrents and, being so far forward, we had lost touch with our ration party and there was no food, only hard tack and water.

It was our hope that when morning came we would be

relieved but no such luck! Instead we had Jerry back, making a series of counter-attacks which we only stopped with the greatest of difficulty and twice they almost overran our position. By mid-morning our supporting troops arrived, so we were relieved and could now make our way back to our own lines. This was easier said than done, for with all the fighting going on around us we could not extricate ourselves without sustaining further casualties. I saw many of the lads fall before we regained our own lines.

What a relief to be back and out of the fighting, with a meal and nice hot cup of tea to drink, a time to relax and sleep. Alas, it was not to be. Come nightfall we were dished out with a supply of ammo and sent forward once more! It turned out that the Germans had taken back a lot of their lost ground and were coming back towards us. We were sent out to stop the rot.

The fighting at Loos was savage and bitter, both sides suffering heavy losses. In the first three days of fighting our battalion lost 372 men. The Germans fought with great determination and recaptured a lot of lost ground, so in the end it was back to the usual stalemate situation once more.

For the remainder of September through to October the slogging match continued, achieving very little except adding to the mounting casualty list. Assaults were made on the Hohenzollern Redoubt and Hulluch, the latter place proving particularly costly to us when we made an attack on 13th October. Our Battalion was in support of the Black Watch, who were ordered to take the German front line trench and were to follow up and pass through to take Hulluch. Preceded by gas and smoke, the Black Watch went into the attack and reports came back that they had been successful. However, these proved to be incorrect since the enemy wire was unbroken and the attack came to a standstill. Worst still, the Black Watch was in retreat. Due to the mist and smoke, vision was seriously impaired and we could see nothing of the battle from our support line. A decision was made to send us forward , so off we went into No Man's Land, only to be met by the Black Watch and men of other outfits coming back at a rush. In the chaos that ensued, men of all regiments jammed into our forward trenches and it was not long before Jerry took stock of the situation and shelled our positions with all the guns he had available. 'A' Company in particular was badly hit, losing nearly sixty men.

We were told later that day that we would continue to attack at first light in the morning. So on the morrow we mounted the fire-steps ready to go forward again but barely had some of us climbed the parapet than we got a recall signal, which undoubtedly saved a lot of lives.

That the Battle of Loos was a failure there is no doubt. We lost nearly 60,000 men without gaining hardly any ground, yet attack and counter-attack continued for the rest of the year - albeit on a much smaller scale and without a major gain by either side.

It was during this period that we returned to some sort of normality, if you can describe life in the trenches as being normal! What I mean to say is that we saw little action and were either in support or reserve. We did twelve days in the trenches and six in billets. Our main task was to clean up the trenches we occupied, for they were full of dead bodies and other debris, not having been touched since September's battles.

We spent the winter of 1915/16 in the trenches near Hulluch, a sector of the line we were destined to hold for the next six months. With the weather bad (plenty of rain and snow), I decided to volunteer for mining duties and at least by so doing get some shelter from the elements.

Tunnelling was a rather laborious job, as we dug out the soil with our bayonets. Luckily it was of a chalky nature so the actual digging was not as difficult as one would imagine. The tricky part was to stay undetected, for the Germans had listening posts out searching for signs of such activity. We used to work perhaps for half an hour, then it would be our turn to listen out for the enemy who were perhaps engaged on the same business as ourselves.

The idea behind all this was to build a tunnel under the enemy's line or well out into No Man's Land, then pack the end of it with explosives and at a given time detonate it. The infantry meanwhile would be waiting to make a dash for the crater as soon as an explosion took place. By so doing they would gain ground or, if possible, press on and breach the opposing defences.

I enjoyed this spell of work with the New Zealand Mining Company. Our only real danger was being discovered. If an enemy tunnel was located, a counter-tunnel would be pushed out to meet it and when the tunnels came close together, an explosive charge would be let off to seal the opposing tunnel and hopefully catch the miners at work. This type of operation called for a lot of skill and a great deal of luck. Of course the enemy also did the same thing to us but fortunately, despite spending a good deal of time underground, I never did see a mine go up. When the tunnel I was working on exploded, I was out on rest many miles back.

With all this tunnelling and sap building in progress, the trenches were sometimes only as little as thirty or forty yards apart. Even though we were in close proximity to the enemy, it seemed that neither side were interested in pressing for an advantage, so it was quiet generally. It could have been that after the autumn battles both sides had exhausted themselves.

Behind the trenches we had reinforced the old derelict miners' houses, which gave us protection from the weather and to some degree, enemy fire.

Around this time we came out of the line and were billeted to a place called Sailly La Bourse, approximately two miles south-east of Bethune. I was walking along the road when I noticed a soldier digging a hole in an orchard adjoining a large gable-ended house with all its windows blown out. It occurred to me that a court martial had been held there and a prisoner had been sentenced to death. As it happened, my billet was only a short distance away from the orchard and when I awoke the next morning I heard signs of activity going on close by. Remembering what I had seen the previous day, I thought, "This sounds like a firing squad being organised."

Getting out of bed, I made my way to the orchard and sure enough, there was the prisoner just being led out of the house; bound, and with a white disc over his heart. The six man firing squad carried out their duty and then the APM (Assistant Provost Marshall) went up to the soldier and made sure of the job by shooting him in the head with his revolver. It was said later that the dead man was from the East Kents and had been found guilty of desertion. Rumour also had it that his father, an ambulance driver, was based only a few kilometres away but had been refused permission to see his son before he died.

In the early months of 1916 the Germans mounted a massive attack against the French at Verdun. The ensuing battle accounted for thousands of deaths on both sides but by May the German troops, led by their Crown Prince, were gaining the ascendancy. To take the pressure off of Verdun, the French General Joffre asked Haigh, the British General, to go over to the offensive in the Somme sector. The date for this counterstroke was scheduled for 1st July.

German positions on the Somme and Ancre were strong by nature and had been strengthened by every device known to their military engineers. Villages had been made into fortresses, two elaborate trench systems had been dug and there was an abundance of wire. The chalk countryside lent itself to the construction of deep dugouts and there was also a collection of redoubts at points of tactical importance. As the Germans had been practically undisturbed in this area for nearly two years, their local knowledge stood them in good stead.

When the fighting began, the British Army had mixed fortunes, making in-roads on one flank and failing on the other, but as the battle gained momentum, reserves came flooding in from other sectors. This is when we got our new marching orders.

On 5th July we left the trenches at Loos and marched on to Lillers, where we entrained for Albert in the south. From there we marched to a location called Mametz Wood, near Contalmaison, in support of the 2nd Brigade.

By the middle of the month we had seen plenty of action and had suffered casualties from both shelling and gas. In conjunction with the Loyal North Lancs and the Royal Sussex, we attacked the German line near Poziers, hoping to make a breakthrough. It was not to be.... it turned out to be another shambles, as our troops got mixed up and failed to make a concerted attack. The Germans had another field day as once more their Maxims mowed us down. To cap it all, next day they heavily shelled our lines and we lost even more men.

So ended our first spell on the Somme. When we were relieved and marched back to Albert, we found at roll call that another 268 officers and men had been lost.

On Talavera Day, the 28th July, we were still out of the line. Talavera Day was always celebrated by the Battalion in remembrance of a battle that the 48th Regiment of Foot (1st Battalion Northamptonshire Regiment) fought in the Peninsula War.

We made the best of our rest at Franvillers. An added bonus was that we did not return to the front straightway, but were sent on a fortnight's training at Henencourt Wood, where a new draft of men, fresh out from home, would join us to replace the men that had been lost in the last battle.

These drafts in the first two years of war were usually filled by men from the county, but as the conflict dragged on, less and less Northants men joined our ranks and we had people from various parts of the UK. Many of the newcomers were North Country men or from Norfolk. As for officer replacements, some were fresh out of Sandhurst or Officer Training Units and the only experienced officers came from other regiments and were seconded to us.

On our return to the front, we were placed in reserve close to High Wood, which was occupied by the enemy. Two days later we were taken out of reserve and went over onto the attack.

From 14th August onwards the fighting was bitter and continuous, both sides at times going over onto the offensive and all the time we strived to take High Wood. The Germans gave as good as they got and fought for every inch of the ground. It was probably the worst period for sustained savagery that I experienced on the Western Front.

Eventually we did gain and consolidate a position in High Wood, but at high cost: 400 casualties in the first seven days of fighting!

One sad loss to me personally was the death of my mate 'Noggy' Bray. For two years Noggy had been behind the lines working on the 'cooker', a cushy number, but for some reason of his own he volunteered to rejoin the infantry. I remember that we were near Ovillers on a working party marching up to the lines. Noggy's section were way up in front of us when they were unlucky enough to receive a direct hit from a 'Jack Johnson' (a heavy artillery shell which made a very large crater when it hit the ground). In all, twenty-three men were killed or wounded, Noggy being one of the former. We buried our dead comrades in the crater and carried the wounded back to the nearest Aid Post.

It was with relief that we left the line on 11th September when we handed over to a London territorial battalion and made our way back to Bescourt Wood.

Thinking back to the times spent on the Western Front, it is hard to believe how callous we became. Dead men meant nothing to us and we treated corpses as a butcher would a carcase of meat. Often in the trenches during or after a battle, scores of bodies would be found and in order to clear a way through, we would throw the corpses out into No Man's Land. In fact, in a way we despised death, with its corruption and stench that was with you all the time except in the sleeping hours.

One example of our disregard for the dead happened on the Somme. In one of the trenches there was a dead German soldier sitting upright on a fire-step. He had been there for weeks and we had to pass him regularly on the way to our position. Every time I went by I used to shake his hand and say "What are you sitting there for, you silly bugger?" It seems so cold and bizarre now that I am relating it, but at the time life was so cheap that only by being hard could we keep our sanity. We used to crack macabre jokes to try and impress on each other our immunity to the horrors we found ourselves in and pretend that our morale was still holding up. It was unfeeling of us perhaps, but it was the only way to keep cheerful in this living hell we found ourselves condemned to.

During my next spell in the line I happened to meet up with my brother-in-law, Joe Walden. I was talking to an artillery man and mentioned Joe's name. He said to me, "This is your lucky day, he's down in the trench over there." Sure enough, Joe was in the support trench with a Stokes mortar battery. As already mentioned, the mortar men lived in the trenches with us and went over the top alongside us, so they earned our respect.

The sector we were now holding was near Hardicourt, a short distance from Flers, a place that would go down in history as the spot where tanks were first used in battle. Many people think that the tank first made its appearance at Cambrai in 1917, but this is incorrect - it was on 15th September 1916 at Flers that British tanks first lumbered into action. Cambrai was more publicised as tanks were used in greater numbers.

We started our attack on the morning of the 15th and for once made good progress and took a lot of ground (up to a mile in one place). Whether the tanks made any impression on the outcome of the battle is debatable. It may be that the advent of the tank boosted some peoples' morale, but speaking for myself, I was totally unimpressed! Forty tanks were detailed to lead the advance but four would not start, many others broke down and only eleven succeeded in crossing the front line. A few of these only joined in the action due to steering troubles. To be fair though, I admit they did cause some consternation to the enemy. The German infantry advancing towards them, not knowing the effectiveness of the tanks' machine-guns (there were two, one on each side), were gunned down.

To me these first tanks seemed cumbersome and archaic. They were small (not much larger than the tractors that you see around these days) but worst of all, they only did three miles per hour at top speed and afforded little protection for the infantry who went out alongside them. It was not possible to get in front of the tanks as they would not be able to use their guns, so you were forced to follow up behind them at a slow walking pace. This meant of course that you were exposed to enemy fire longer than would normally be the case.

The fighting went well for us, which was surprising as it was only on rare occasions that one of our attacks was crowned with success, but of course it goes without saying that this success had to be paid for with the loss of more human lives.

When I eventually returned to our old front line, I met up again with the gunner who I had spoken to previously and he told me that my brother-in-law Joe was a casualty and had been taken back to the field hospital. Later I discovered that Joe had been wounded but had made good recovery. The next time I saw him was when the war had finished and we were both back in Northampton.

It was shortly after this we were relieved by the French Foreign Legion. What a sight they were with bright red trousers, long-tailed grey coats, a type of riding boots and caps with shiny black peaks. To see them you would thought they had just walked off a scene set in Hollywood. I don't know how they fared that winter, but you could only feel sorry for them with the bad weather coming on.

For a few weeks we recuperated in the back areas and it was not until well into November that we went up the line again, this time at Eaucourt L'Abbaye on the Somme. The weather was dreadful and the trenches were water-logged, conditions being as bad as they were at Loos and Givenchy in previous winters. In certain places the trenches were thigh deep in mud and slush and it really got you down.

Dead bodies were everywhere – on the parapets and the ground in front and, worst of all, lying under water at the bottom of the trench, so that you fell or stumbled over them as you made your way through.

In addition, nothing could be cooked in the front trench and obtaining food was a problem. Sometimes it would take four to five hours for the rations to arrive, as they could only be got to us by men carrying them on their backs.

Sickness amongst us was very high too. Most of us suffered in some way or other with trench foot and trench fever, both these complaints being prevalent. Frostbite was another hazard and the whale oil was of little help.

In a period of six weeks, 14 men were killed and 39 wounded by enemy action, but hundreds more were out of the line due to sickness. Even a new draft of nearly 500 men barely brought the battalion up to strength.

The ruins of the village of Ovillers in 1916 and a captured German trench in the chalk.

Sorting out the packs of the dead and wounded for letters and personal effects to send to relatives. Horse and motor ambulances can be seen in the background.
South of Gillemont, September 1916.

Sentry on duty in winter.

Soldiers in No Man's Land making their way through mine craters and shell holes.

Germans listening out for mining activities.

Troops in a captured German trench, reversing the defences in case of a counter-attack.

A mine crater – notice the entrance to the deep German dugout.

The remains of a village near Mametz after shelling.

Joe Walden, Frank's brother-in-law, who served in the Royal Artillery but shared the discomforts of trench life with his Stokes mortar battery.

Troops joining up shell-holes to make a defensive position.

A knocked-out tank. Notice the thinness of the armour plate.

The British 'Push' near Flers, 1916.

Stunted trees in the fight for a wood.
Notice the sap dug into the wood to aid advance.

An advanced dressing station, Martinuich (Somme).
Battle of Flers-Courcelette, 15-22 September 1916.

Battle of Morval, near Guinchy, September 1916.
Troops in reserve awaiting orders to attack.

Horses stuck in the mud after rain on the Somme.

5. THE FINAL YEARS

The beginning of 1917 found us resting near Albert, if you can call living in bell tents in a snow-covered field during the extremely bitter January weather resting! To us though, after the conditions we had to endure in our last location, this seemed like paradise.

Our next turn in the trenches did not occur until February, when we took over from the French at Mericourt. It was a fairly quiet sector and we were more than pleased for the respite, but in March there were rumours that the Germans were in retreat and every day we expected that we would be pushing forward once more.

What was really happening was that the Germans, after the big Somme battles of the previous autumn, wanted to straighten their line where a large salient had developed which made them vulnerable to attack. They had prepared a strong position in their rear, which became known as the Line. This line of defence had been strengthened with block-houses, strong points in depth and masses of wire. It was considered to be the answer to any future attack from the Allied Armies.

This German retreat, or perhaps retirement would be a better word to use, started during March. It seemed that neither side was anxious to make a fight of it and our army advanced cautiously behind the Germans. We followed up for miles, passing through the old German lines at a leisurely pace. It was marvellous to see green fields once again but Jerry had left behind a trail of destruction: all the hamlets and villages had been destroyed; the houses looted, burned or booby-trapped; live stock driven off; and even the fruit trees in the orchards had been ring-barked.

At last we arrived at the Hindenburg Line and warfare became static again. It then became a question of us digging-in and waiting to see what the next phase would be. Thankfully we had little interference from the enemy and it continued this way until we left the line in May.

We did not re-enter the trenches again until the end of June. This time we were right up to the sea front at Nieuport. All was very quiet and we were hoping for a restful stay by the sea. It didn't quite turn out that way however.

Only part of the battalion was occupying the front line, a collection of fox holes and breastworks in amongst the sand dunes; the rest of us were in reserve further back. Then disaster struck on 10th July.

The following action, which became known as the 'Battle of the Dunes', opened early in the morning with a bombardment by heavy artillery and the barrage continued for the best part of the day. It was not unlike the Somme all over again, only this time it was Jerry that was making the running. Our own artillery was unable to give us much assistance as they were very short in numbers and it seemed that the shelling was all one way. As the day wore on the German guns caused havoc amongst the lads up front, killing and burying many of them, whilst the support areas also took a terrible bashing from the shelling.

Our men were penned-in in a very small area, which proved to be a death trap. No serious fighting had occurred here since the war began and it was probably for this reason that the terrain had never been carefully studied.

The sector in question was only a mile wide, with the sea left and a large dyke on the right. This dyke joined the canal, which was half a mile in the rear and ran parallel to the front line. Three makeshift bridges were placed over the canal and these were the only link between the men at the front and those at the rear. Of course, the Germans were well aware of the vulnerability of these bridges and they were quickly destroyed in the first phase of the battle.

When the assault started, it was led by a first class Marine Division, who soon penetrated our defences. The lads of the battalion who had survived put up a gallant fight but bravery was not enough and they were overwhelmed. Only eight men managed to escape by swimming across the Yser Canal.

This was probably the battalion's greatest loss, as in the final count it was found that 20 officers and 570 men had been either killed, wounded or taken prisoner. I am glad to say that I was not one of those involved on that particular day!

After this disaster it was not until November that we were called upon to do any further fighting, for we had to make good our losses with new reinforcements. Then it was training and drill to lick us into shape for another round with the enemy.

About this time, for some reason or another, many of our men were placed at the disposal of other units and I, with others, went to join our 5th Battalion which was then based at Handécourt. The 5th were a pioneer battalion, engaged at that time on road and rail work just behind the lines.

My new job was to act as runner for the CO Colonel Trent and his adjutant Captain Cathcart of the Headquarters staff. It was a job that I did not relish much as it was not without its special dangers. The carrying of messages in No Man's Land was no picnic. Twice when I was in the support trenches with the Colonel we came under an accurate bombardment from heavy artillery which gave us many anxious moments. Luckily we came through it all without a scratch.

Colonel Trent was a professional soldier of many years service and a real gent. I got on with him quite well as he was an approachable officer and one you could share a joke with. Captain Cathcart was also a nice kind of chap and a confirmed fatalist! (*Before the war I believe he was an engineer and had a firm in London.*) He was a man without fear, or at least I never saw him show it. Sometimes it was my duty to accompany the Captain when he went round on inspection. He would walk along the parapet above the trenches or out in No Man's Land unconcernedly and would say to me, "You keep to the trench James if you wish, there is no need to follow me." - I didn't!

Most of the officers I knew were brave men. I think a lot of it was to do with the way they were brought up. Coming as they did mainly from the upper classes, they were taught from an early age that they were destined to be the leaders of men and must at all times show fortitude and keep a stiff upper lip in the face of adversity. Above all they must, by personal example, set standards that others might follow. It was my opinion that the officers were more afraid of showing weakness in front of their men than they were of facing the enemy.

To return to the fighting; at that time our troops had made big advances into enemy held territory. The Germans, having shortened their lines, were now holding the defensive position known as the Hindenburg Line and we were now occupying what had been the old German trenches, which were some miles behind the Front, where our lads were still pushing forward. So all was quiet as we were out of the action entirely. The only activity in our sector was when three naval guns were brought up from the rear and sited in No Man's Land, just in front of our dug-outs.

One morning I was up and abroad early, when I heard scuffling and noises in front of our trench, so I got up onto the fire-step to investigate. What a shock I had - there were the Germans manhandling the three guns! I could hardly believe my eyes! How could they have reached our Headquarters without us being aware of an attack? I ran to tell the Colonel who was sleeping in a dugout close by.

"Colonel!" I said.

"Yes", he replied, "What do you want?"

I answered, "If you want to get away you had better be quick, the Germans are here."

He said, "James you must be bloody mad!", to which I answered, "So will you be when you come and take a look."

He came out of his quarters, looked over the parapet and could hardly take in what he saw.

"Good God," he said, "every man for himself!" That was the only time that I heard those words used throughout the war.

There was a mate with me at that time called Jack Lenton and we made a dash for it. There was a deep railway cutting nearby (similar to the one at Roade but with more of a slope), so we ran for this, accompanied by another soldier. (I think he was from the Norfolks by the look of his badge.)

"If we can get over the brow of this incline," I shouted, "we should be out of sight of the enemy".

Imagine our surprise when we reached the top to see the

Germans coming up to meet us! I often think about this episode and have a quiet laugh to myself, although it wasn't funny at the time. We must have looked like one of those chase scenes from an old Hollywood comedy.

"Let's give ourselves up", said Jack.

"No, bugger it, I'm not giving in." I said.

We set off in a different direction and had at this time lost the other soldier - we never saw him again so he probably surrendered to the Germans.

With all the cratered and shell-torn ground around us, we managed to elude our pursuers and luck was with us for we had run in the right direction and it was not long before we met up with the Military Police.

The Military Police were normally stationed well behind the lines; it was their job to direct traffic and watch out for deserters. In the case of a retreat, such as this was, they stopped all stragglers at gunpoint and formed them up in a defensive position.

We were rounded up with many other men from various units and directed to a nearby ditch to form a line of defence. As we lay there a section of cavalry went by us to try and stop the German advance. The man who sent them forward deserved to be shot. To be sent over broken ground littered with barbed wire, of which there was plenty lying around, and to face up to machine-gun and rifle fire was suicidal. Needless to say, the charge was a complete fiasco and it was pitiful to hear the cries of the wounded horses as they lay out there dying on the field!

The German advance petered out after a few days, but they did manage to retake most of the ground that they had lost in earlier battles.

Although I did not witness it myself, some of the lads mentioned afterwards of the bravery of one of the officers - I think they said it was a Lieutenant Fowler. According to reports, we were being overrun and he managed to take cover in a sunken road. The Germans were leading prisoners and the Colonel's horse back to their lines. He shot the guards and got the men to join him. I never did hear the end of the story or even if he survived, but he certainly deserved a medal for his courage.

Colonel Trent during the fighting managed to rally a force of cooks, engineers and men who were normally non-combatants to hold a position named Revlon Farm, which he did successfully until relieved by the Coldstream Guards.

By April of 1918 we were stationed in the Cuinchy sector, almost at the same place we had occupied in 1915. It was an area that had been relatively undisturbed since that time. At least no big battles had been fought there and civilians still lived and worked within a very short distance of our front line.

As we took up our positions in the line at Festubert, we were unaware that the Germans were poised ready to start a general offensive against the British Army, scheduled to start before dawn on the following day.

In the front and on our flank, the Portuguese were holding the line. They were fresh troops who had not been under fire before, so were an unknown quantity and unproven in battle. This must have been on the enemy's mind too, for when the blow fell, the Portuguese proved to be the weak link in our defences - and the Germans certainly capitalised on it!

The morning of the attack, the 9th April, there was a heavy mist and visibility was down to a few yards. We knew that an attack was underway by the hail of shells falling in front of us, so we crouched down in the trench waiting for our turn to come. Shortly after we were alerted by our sentries that the Germans were almost on top of us. What had really happened was that the Portuguese line had broken and the men were streaming back in disorder. It was a sad fact that the Portuguese uniform was similar to that of the Germans, even to the type of helmet that they wore, so when these soldiers appeared out of the mist, we shot them down and must have killed many of their number.

It was an eerie sort of situation we were in. After the first bout of firing our front was clear, but all around us was the sound of battle and we could not see a thing. All we could do was to wait and hope we had been overlooked by the enemy. Later we learnt that the Germans had bypassed our positions, hoping to come round the back of us and cut us off after dealing with the Portuguese.

The Germans captured Givenchy but were counter-attacked by other regiments and pushed back to their starting point. This was not the case in other parts of the line for the German Army made great gains and succeeded in pushing our army back towards the channel ports, taking Albert in the process.

In our sector, after attacks by both sides, the fighting slackened and it was left to the artillery to continue the war. But that did not mean we got away without casualties, for the month's losses were far from being insignificant - they exceeded the 200 mark!

The big advance by the Germans continued throughout the months of May and June, in the course of which they gained a lot of territory, captured thousands of men and took over vast masses of war material and supplies. The most important thing of all was that they failed to break the British Army and reach the coast to cut us off from the French.

In the end the German offensive ran out of steam and they were halted. The French meanwhile, under General Foche, had launched a big counter-stroke between the Aisne and the Marne in July, which boosted our morale for not only had we taken all that the enemy could throw at us, but we had stopped him in his tracks and now our Allies were on the attack once more.

By August the British Army had recovered its strength and was ready to take its part in the new offensive, which took place along the whole Western Front. The Germans were in retreat and although they fought bravely, they were unable to break our momentum once it got started and which never slackened. Even the renowned Hindenburg Line failed to stop us and we never lost the initiative until the cease-fire stopped all operations on 11th November 1918.

Our involvement in this final phase of the war started in September when we were called upon to lend support to General Rawlinson's 4th Army, fighting its way through the St. Quentin sector. On the first part of the journey we travelled in style by motor buses but it was not long before we used 'Shanks's pony' again.

Once we met up with the enemy we made good progress

and it was fighting all the way. One night was spent in a wood near Vermand and just when we thought it would be peaceful and we might get a good night's rest, Jerry bombarded us with gas shells and followed up by sending aircraft over to bomb us! Next morning we checked for casualties and found three men dead and twenty-two others wounded. This was about the same number that we lost on the following day, when we came under shell-fire again.

Presently we were called upon to make an attack on the village of Berthaucourt with four tanks to assist us. It was early morning when we were assembled to go forward into the attack and once we did, the German Maxims had the last say. It was a complete failure! As for our tank escort, one missed it's directions and did not arrive in time, two were put out of action by shell-fire before the advance began, and the remaining machine was last seen disappearing in the wrong direction, away from the scene of battle! Later in the day the 60th Rifles came to our rescue and succeeded in driving the Germans back. This unpleasant day's work cost our battalion dearly. We lost over 200 men in the action.

Soon we were sent back in reserve for a short period and it was mid-October before we joined the line at Bohain, near Le Cateau. This time we were going to push on towards the Sambre Canal and take Wassigny.

On the morning of 17th October, we made our way forward towards the Germans in fog so thick that we could not see where we were going. All we could do was to follow the officers and NCOs who were in front and had to go forward on compass bearings, or so I was told.

At about 10.30am the fog lifted and we found ourselves in a village by the name of La Vallée Mulatre, the Germans at one end and us at the other. Fighting for the village continued into the afternoon with neither side gaining the upper hand. It was only when we put down some heavy shelling that Jerry withdrew and we were able to push on to our original objective - Wassigny. This cost us another 100 men.

Two days later we marched north to Mazinheim, some two and a half miles away, where we were to meet up with American troops for the first time. What a sight - these fresh looking lads, all raring to go. We could hardly believe it! They showered us with gifts of chocolate, cigarettes, rations, etc., saying, "We won't need these, we are off to Berlin in the morning," and, "OK you guys, which way to the shooting gallery?"

I thought, "Keep on coming lads, you're the ones we are looking for."

During the night the American positions took a pasting from Jerry's Howitzers and they also had a visit from the German Air Force. I met some of the Americans later, coming back up the line and I said to one of them, "Where are you off to then?"

He replied, "I'm going back to report sick. I've bloody well had enough."

Our stay with the Yanks was very brief and soon we joined up with the Royal Sussex and 60th Rifles for the advance to the Sambre Canal. We crossed the canal on 4th November but it was no easy task and was contested every inch of the way. Once we had crossed, our adversaries seemed to have little fight left in them and retreated as soon as darkness fell.

At the time none of us could have guessed that this would be the last time we would be in action, but the writing was on the wall for all to see and most of us I think realised that the end was not far away.

In the course of our advance we liberated many villages that had been in German hands almost throughout the war and at one such village we found the population almost starving. Our vet helped out in one small way; when he inspected our baggage animals he found one of the mules unfit for further work so he shot it and gave the carcase to the villagers, who were most grateful. We met two ladies in this village who lived together in a big house, one was a school mistress and the other the wife of the Station Master at Valenciennes. They invited us to dinner that evening to feast on the mule but we politely refused, not that we were adverse to eating the meat (for I am sure it would have tasted much better than our rations), but because we did not wish to deprive them of any food.

Whilst we were there we met a girl who was about

seventeen years of age who could speak some English. She told us that she had been deported by the Germans to work in one of their factories but had escaped to this village where her uncle lived, not daring to return to her own parents' village in case she was deported once again.

Another lad of around the same age had spent the war years hiding in the roof of his parents' home. He was over six feet tall, very thin, puffed up and with a complexion the colour of flour. This was due to the fact that he never emerged during daylight hours and only rarely at night with a curfew in force.

Shortly after leaving this village we ended up in Valenciennes, billeted in a brewery for the night. I was with Bobby Armstrong, a man who kept a shop in Towcester. As we were walking through this brewery, Bobby said to one of the men working there, "Bonsoir, Monsieur."

The man replied, "It's all right mate, you don't have to practice your French on me, I come from Birmingham."

We should have talked to him further, but we never did. I suppose we thought that he might have been a deserter and did not wish to get involved. I am sure that man would have had a tale to tell — especially since this town had been in enemy territory up until two days before.

It was whilst we were in Valenciennes that we heard that an armistice had been agreed. We happened to get into conversation with an old French couple who we met in the street. They spoke a bit of English and told us that the cease-fire had been set for eleven o'clock the following day. This was the first news we had received, having heard nothing from our HQ.

On the last day of war we were just over the Belgian frontier, marching along a road and wondering what would happen at eleven o'clock. Nothing did! The guns continued firing for a while afterwards and I suppose it was nearer twelve noon before the last sounds of firing died away and silence prevailed at last.

As we rested by the roadside, a squadron of artillery came past us and we were amazed at how spick and span they looked. It was pretty obvious that they had had plenty of notice that the war was going to end, for the horses were groomed and harnesses and brasses polished. They could easily have been taken for a squadron attending a parade.

Now that the war was at an end we thought our next move would be home and demob, but the army thought otherwise and our long march started to the Rhine. We followed on the heels of the German Army, who were making their way back to their own country. Our progress being most leisurely, we rarely glimpsed our former enemy, but sometimes Uhlan cavalry would be spotted on the horizon, who were acting as rear guards on the German line of march.

Our journey to Duisdorf, near Bonn, lasted for over a month and it was not without its moments. Although we were now officially at peace, the Germans still acted as if they were at war. Booby traps and delayed-action mines were left at all key crossing points like bridges, crossroads and railway crossings, so impeding our march. Villages and hamlets had been pillaged too and property burnt or destroyed.

In the early part of our travels we liberated hundreds of prisoners of war, took masses of war material and were welcomed everywhere we went. However, on reaching the Ardennes, the population proved very hostile towards us. When we tried to get billets for the night they would say that there was a Scarlet Fever epidemic in their village or that there was a Foot and Mouth outbreak amongst their cattle. At night you needed to be on your guard in case in the morning you found that the harness used by the transport animals had been cut up.

Travel in the Ardennes was very difficult. There had been lots of rain, the roads were terrible (often proving to be only forest tracks) and the hills created problems for our transport waggons.

Once we crossed the German frontier things improved considerably. The weather still remained bad, with rain and some snow, but the attitude of the civilian population was much better and we were treated with respect and civility. Villages were also much cleaner and well kept - so different to those we had known hitherto in France and Belgium. But of course, in this region villages were far removed from the battlefields and were untouched by the ravages of war.

Duisdorf, our final destination, was reached on Christmas Eve. It was too late for us to organise a party but we did make up for it on New Year's Eve when we held a celebration in the local Town Hall.

Most of us were billeted out with the civilians in the town and what a pleasure it was to be sleeping in a real bed again, a luxury that some of us had had to forfeit for several years. Our hosts were almost at starvation point, so we helped them out when we could by supplying them with some of our own rations (which incidentally were excellent now the fighting was over). Through this help, many friendships were formed. We also met some of the Germans who had fought against us and discussed past times with them. There was no animosity, for we were all fellow sufferers of the same conflict.

Early in the new year of 1919 I was included in a draft going back to England. So ended my stay on the Continent; glad to be going back home to Blighty, thankfully all in one piece!

******

German blockhouses in front of the Menin road.

One of the make-shift bridges over the Yser Canal which was destroyed by German artillery in the first phase of the Battle of the Dunes on 10th July 1917. The 1st Northants lost 20 officers and 570 men – only 8 men escaped by swimming back across the canal.

Tank trapped in a ditch near Famcourt, 1918.

King George V with men of the Northants 1st Battalion near Zillebeke, July 1917, just before the Third Battle of Ypres. The battalion mascot is a twelve year-old Belgian orphan – he went about with the transport section and later joined a Belgian Regimental Band.

Irish Guardsmen attending a wounded German in a trench.
The Battle of Pilckem Ridge, 31st July 1917.

A 'Tommy' giving a light to a badly wounded German soldier lying in a ditch. Battle of Pilckem Ridge, 31st July 1917 – Third Battle of Ypres.

British troops moving forward over shell-torn ground near Pilckem, 16th August 1917.

British propaganda photo of 1918 showing how the Germans were supposedly 'scraping the barrel' to fill their depleted units.

Men of the 1st Battalion resting in a front line trench at Molain, near Vaux Andigny, before the advance to the Sambre Canal on 17th October 1918. The attack was made in dense fog and was partly successful with 8 guns and 30 machine-guns taken, but the casualties for the battalion were 14 killed and 84 wounded or gassed.

5th Northamptons making a road to the Front.

All that remained of the 5th Battalion at the Armistice of those who went out with the Battalion in 1915. They belong chiefly to the Transport.

EPILOGUE

Most families suffered a tragedy of some sort or another during The Great War and some villages lost a whole generation of young men. Incredibly all the James brothers and their father survived the conflict intact and they lived to a ripe old age. For his part in the war Frank received the 1914/15 Star, British War and Victory medals.

Frank was demobilised in 1919 and joined the Gas Company in Northampton as a fitter, where he remained until he retired. As part of his job he had to travel to make safe gas supplies and he was one of the first to enter Coventry after the Blitz of the Second World War. After all the devastation he had seen in the trenches, he claimed that he had never seen anything as bad as Coventry.

He married his sweetheart Lily Gibbins and they had one daughter, Olive, but she was a sick child and sadly died at the age of seven. The doctors told them that her illness was a result of Frank being gassed during the war.

Frank lived in Nursery Lane, Kingsthorpe, Northampton up until his death in 1987, at the age of ninety-one. Even in his nineties Frank was a very active man, spending much time on his garden and allotment and helping out on the farm of a friend who lived in Harlestone. Frank was also a keen cyclist and motorist, using both methods of transport almost up until the time of his death. He was a familiar sight in Kingsthorpe, riding his bike down Mill Lane; a tall upright man of six feet or more in height whose face belied his grand age.

The Great War had been a terrible event that must have permanently affected the lives of all those who survived it, though most of them preferred to keep their memories to themselves. Let us hope that Frank's story will help us remember the brutality and suffering they endured, Lest We Forget.

Frank with his wife Lil and daughter Olive (c.1925).

Frank (right) in 1986 aged 90 with brother Arthur (86) and youngest sister Ivy (82).

Ron James

POEMS

The Battle of Blenheim
By R Southey

They say it was a shocking sight
After the field was won.
For many thousand bodies here
Lay rotting in the sun:
But things like that, you know, must be
After a famous victory . . .

'But what good came of it at last?'
Quoth little Peterkin.
'Why, that I cannot tell,' said he
'But 'twas a famous victory.'

The General
By Siegfried Sassoon

"Good morning; good morning!" the General said
When we met him last week on the way to the line.
Now the soldiers he smiled at are most of 'em dead,
And we're cursing his staff for incompetent swine.
"He's a cheery old card," grunted Harry to Jack
As they slogged up to Arras with rifle and pack.

*

But he did for them both with his plan of attack.

In Flanders' Fields
By John McCrae, 1915

In Flanders fields the poppies blow
Between the crosses, row on row,
That mark our place: and in the sky
The larks, still bravely singing, fly
Scarce heard amid the guns below.
We are the dead. Short days ago
We lived, felt dawn, saw sunset glow,
Loved and were loved, and now we lie
In Flanders' fields.
Take up our quarrel with the foe;
To you from failing hands we throw
The torch; be yours to hold it high,
If ye break faith with us who die
We shall not sleep, though poppies grow
In Flanders' Fields.

Menin Gate Memorial at Ypres, Belgium.

APPENDIX

DESERTERS

The first soldier to be executed on the Western Front in 1916 was a 19 year old deserter in 1st Northamptonshire Regiment, Private John Dennis from Cheetham Hill near Manchester. When tried he stated in his defence that heavy shelling had affected his mind. However this argument did not convince the court who were later to hear that Dennis was under a suspended sentence of two years imprisonment with hard labour for a previous offence of desertion. (The account given by Judge Babington maintained that Dennis was of previous good character.)

Dennis' trial took place on 3rd December and the subsequent 58 day delay in confirming and then carrying out the sentence was the longest of the war. On 19th December 1915 Sir Douglas Haig replaced Sir John French as Commander-in-Chief of the British Expeditionary Force on the Western Front. Private Dennis was the first of 253 soldiers upon whom Haig decided that the sentence of death would be carried out. (Eleven of these 253 death sentences were for murder.) Throughout the delay Private Dennis remained with his unit until, at 7.10am on 30th January 1916, he was executed by a firing squad of ten men from his battalion.

The battalion war diary, kept on active service, recorded that it was thought to be the first case of an execution in the regiment since the Peninsular days. Dennis was buried at Lillers Communal Cemetery, France.

Towards the end of February another soldier from the Northamptonshire Regiment was executed. He was the second man from 1st Battalion to be executed in 1916 and this was the fourth execution in 1 Division in just two months. No other soldier from the Northamptonshire Regiment was executed during the remainder of the war, indicating just how sporadic the use of the death penalty could be. Like his comrade before him, the doomed man's offence related to events in 1915.

On 7th October 1915 the battalion had taken over newly captured German trenches near Mazingarbe. After a preliminary bombardment the next day, the Germans attacked 'en masse'. The battalion held its ground and the enemy were beaten back, after which the men were ordered to dig trenches and consolidate their positions. The next evening, the night of 10th October, the men were busy bringing up gas cylinders in preparation for an attack. Private John Jones, sensing that more bloodshed was soon to follow, made off the next day whilst on sentry duty in a support trench.

The following month he was arrested in Bethune, but on 14th December he managed to escape by a subterfuge. He remained at liberty until 3rd February and was tried a week later. He told the court that he had deserted because his platoon sergeant continually victimised him. His length of absence, coupled with his offence of escaping, weighed heavily against him. Other matters, of which the court took no regard, was the fact that he was only 21 years old and the father of a young child.

On 24th February Jones became the third soldier to be executed in the abattoir at Mazingarbe. Like the previously executed soldiers, he was buried in the nearby Communal Cemetery, but for a reason that is not clear he is buried in an isolated grave quite separate from the other British military burials. The battalion war diary does not record the execution and hence it would seem probable that he was shot by a firing squad comprised of men from a battalion other than his own. The burial officer may well have decided that because of the manner in which he met his death, that Jones should be buried separately.

INDEX

A

Aircraft, 25, 93
Aisne, 92
Albert, 65, 66, 86, 92
Americans, 49, 50, 93, 94
Ancre, 65
Ardennes, 96
Armstrong, Bobby, 95
Army, 4th, 92
Arras, 22, 110
Artillery, 25, 26, 29, 30, 37, 41, 46,
　47, 60, 67, 78, 87, 88, 92, 95, 99
Aubers Ridge, 28, 29, 34, 45, 60

B

Battalion, 1st, 12, 66, 101, 106, 112
Battalion, 2nd, 26
Battalion, 5th, 88, 107
Battle of Blenheim, 110
Battle of Flers, 83
Battle of Loos, 60, 63
Battle of Morval, 84
Battle of Neuve Chapelle, 28, 34
Battle of Pilckem Ridge, 102, 103
Battle of the Dunes, 87, 99
Battle of Ypres, 101, 103
Bavarians, 49
Berthaucourt, 93
Bescourt Wood, 67
Bethune, 24, 25, 32, 44, 64, 113
Black Watch, 62
Bohain, 93
Bray, 'Noggy', 12, 66, 67
Brigade, 2nd, 65

C

Cambrai, 68
Cathcart, Captain, 88
Cavalry, 90, 96
Coldstream Guards, 91
Company, A, 63
Company, B, 29
Company, D, 29
Contalmaison, 65
Cuinchy, 91

D

Dennis, John, 112
Deserters, 45, 90, 95, 112
Dickson, Captain, 28, 32
Division, 1st, 61, 112
Duisdorf, 96, 97

E

East Kents, 65
Eaucourt L'Abbaye, 69
Etaples, 22

F

Far Cotton, 11, 12
Festubert, 27, 91
Flers, 68, 81, 83
Foche, General, 92
Fowler, L/t, 90
Franvillers, 66
French Foreign Legion, 69
Front Line, 23, 25, 26, 29, 39, 41, 43,

46, 48, 52, 59, 60, 62, 68, 87, 91, 106

G

Gas, 47, 48, 57, 60, 61, 62, 65, 93, 106, 108
Gibbins, Lily, 108, 109
Givenchy, 22, 24, 69, 92
Greenwood, Private, 25
Grenadier Guards, 12
Griffin, farmer, 33
Guinchy, 24, 84

H

Haigh, General, 65
Hardicourt, 68
Henencourt Wood, 66
High Wood, 66
Hindenburg Line, 86, 87, 89, 92
Hohenzollern Redoubt, 62
Hospital, 22, 24, 26, 27, 32, 38, 45, 69
Howitzer, 94
Hulluch, 62, 63
Hunsbury Hill, 8, 10, 11, 14, 33

I

Indian troops, 23

J

James, Alice, 8
James, Arthur, 8, 10, 12, 19, 33, 109
James, Elsie, 8
James, Fred, 8, 10, 12, 17, 33, 47
James, George, 8, 16
James, Ivy, 109
James, Job, 9
James, Lil, 8

James, Mary, 8
James, William, 8, 12, 18
Joffre, General, 65
Jones, John, 113

K

King George V, 101
King's Dragoon Guards, 12
Kingsthorpe, 108
Kislingbury, 9, 10

L

La Bassée, 24, 28
La Vallée Mulatre, 93
Le Cateau, 93
Le Havre, 13
Lenton, Jack, 89
Life Guards, 12, 18
Lille, 24, 28
Lillers, 65, 112
London Artillery Company, 30
Lone Tree Farm, 61
Loos, 59, 60, 61, 62, 63, 65, 69
Loyal North Lancs, 65

M

Mametz Wood, 65
Marine Division, 87
Matthews, Alf, 19
Maxim machine-guns, 30, 66, 93
Mazingarbe, 113
Mazinheim, 93
Mericourt, 86
Military Police, 90
Mills bombs, 29
Milton, 9

N

Neuve Chapelle, 12, 25, 28, 29, 34
New Zealand Mining Company, 64
Nieuport, 87
No Man's Land, 25, 26, 29, 30, 31, 36, 42, 43, 47, 60, 62, 63, 67, 73, 88, 89
Norfolk, 66, 89
Northampton, iii, iv, 7, 9, 12, 15, 19, 21, 32, 46, 69, 107, 108, 112
Northamptonshire Regiment, iv, 12, 15, 66, 112
Northamptonshire Yeomanry, 12, 19, 33

P

Pickering Phipps, 10, 14, 33
Portuguese, 91
Poziers, 65
Prussian Guard, 49

R

Railway, French, 22, 24, 35, 89
Rations, 24, 29, 32, 44, 46, 48, 50, 52, 61, 69, 94, 97
Rawlinson, General, 92
Revlon Farm, 91
Rifles, 60th, 93, 94
Roberts, Frank, 12
Rouen, 27
Royal Artillery, 78
Royal Sussex Regiment, 60, 65, 94

S

Sailly La Bourse, 64
Sambre Canal, 93, 94, 106
Short, Sgt, 27

Somme, 59, 65, 66, 67, 69, 83, 85, 86, 87
Southampton, 13
St John Ambulance, 12, 16
St Quentin, 92
Stokes Mortar, 46, 67, 78

T

Talavera Day, 48, 66
Tanks, 68, 80, 93, 100
Towcester, 10, 33, 95
Trench fever, 44, 69
Trench foot, 23, 24, 44, 69
Trent, Colonel, 88, 91
Tunnels, 63, 64

U

U-Boat, 13, 50
Uhlan, 96

V

Valenciennes, 94, 95
Verdun, 65
Vermand, 93
Vermin, 32, 43

W

Walden, Joe, 67, 69, 78
Wassigny, 93
West Kents, 24
Weymouth, 12, 13
Worley, Arthur, 12

Y

Yser Canal, 88, 99

Printed in Great Britain
by Amazon.co.uk, Ltd.,
Marston Gate.